LEVEL
3

D0404545

Bears

Elizabeth Carney

NATIONAL
GEOGRAPHIC

Washington, D.C.

For Norbert Rosing, who taught me a lot about bears —E.C.

Trade paperback ISBN: 978-1-4263-2444-4
Reinforced library binding ISBN: 978-1-4263-2445-1

The publisher and author gratefully acknowledge the expert content review of this book by Shannon Donahue, executive director, Great Bear Foundation, and the literacy review of this book by Mariam Jean Dreher, professor of reading education, University of Maryland, College Park.

Author's Note: Grizzly bears, brown bears, and big bears called Kodiak bears are all the same species. For the purposes of this book, any reference to brown bears includes all three.

Art Director: Amanda Larsen
Designer: YAY! Design

Captions: The cover photo shows a brown bear in Kainuu, Finland. A mother polar bear and cub in Manitoba, Canada, are snuggled up on the title page. The table of contents features an Andean bear.

Photo Credits

AL = Alamy; CO = Corbis; GI = Getty Images; MP = Minden Pictures; NGC = National Geographic Creative; NPL = Nature Picture Library; SS = Shutterstock

COVER (Front), Berndt Fischer/Biosphoto; 1 (CTR), Gary Schultz/Design Pics/GI; 3 (LO RT), Mark Newman/MP; 4-5 (UP), Accent Alaska.com/AL; 6 (CTR), Andy Rouse/NPL; 7 (UP RT), Alex Snyder; 7 (LO RT), Hyoung Chang/Denver Post/GI; 8 (UP RT), age fotostock/AL; 8 (LO LE), Paul Williams/NPL; 9 (UP RT), Gerry Ellis/MP/NGC; 9 (LO RT), Gerry Ellis/MP/NGC; 10 (LO), Gerry Ellis/MP/NGC; 11 (UP), Tom Murphy/NGC; 11 (LO), Roy Toft/NGC; 12 (CTR), Gleb Tarro/SS; 13 (LO), Patricio Robles Gil/NGC; 14 (LO), Jim Clare/NPL; 15 (UP), YAY! Design; 16 (CTR), Katherine Feng/MP; 17 (LO), robertharding/AL; 18 (UP), Kennan Ward/CO; 19 (UP RT), Winfried Wisniewski/MP; 19 (LO), Daisy Gilardini/GI; 20 (UP RT), Shvaygert Ekaterina/SS; 20 (CTR), Daniel Eskridge/Stocktrek Images/GI; 20 (LO), Ganesh H Shankar/AL; 21 (UP), Paul Nicklen/NGC; 21 (CTR), Thomas Kitchin & Victoria Hurst/MP; 21 (LO RT), Yva Momatiuk & John Eastcott/MP; 22-23 (UP), Roberta Olenick/GI; 24-25 (CTR), Mark Newman/GI; 26 (LO), Ingo Arndt/CO; 27 (CTR), Dave Garshelis; 28 (UP), Photolibrary/GI; 28 (LO), Signature Message/SS; 29 (UP), Tierfotoagentur/AL; 29 (LO), Juan Carlos Munoz/NPL; 30 (LE), razorpix/AL; 30 (RT), Sergey Krasnoshchokov/SS; 31 (UP LE), Ben Molyneux/AL; 31 (UP RT), Hemis/AL; 31 (LO LE), Treat Davidson/MP; 31 (LO RT), Carolyn Jenkins/AL; 32 (UP), Jeff Pachoud/GI; 32 (CTR), Jeff Pachoud/GI; 33 (CTR), Melissa Groo; 34 (CTR), Ernst Mutchnick/AL; 35 (UP), Michael Hutchinson/MP; 36 (UP), AS400 DB/CO; 37 (RT), Yvette Cardozo/GI; 38 (LO), Kevin Schafer/AL; 39 (UP), Ralph Lee Hopkins/NGC; 40 (UP), AP Photo/CHINATOPIX; 41 (UP), AP Photo/Imaginechina; 41 (LO), Warwick Sloss/NPL; 42 (UP), Stuart O'Sullivan/GI; 43 (LO), Dasha Rosato/AL; 44 (UP), NASA; 44 (CTR), Bernatskaya Oxana/SS; 44 (LO LE), Manfred Ruckszio/SS; 44 (LO RT), Dan Bach Kristensen/SS; 45 (UP RT), Richard Wear/Design Pics/GI; 45 (CTR RT), Matthias Breiter/NGC; 45 (LO LE), blickwinkel/AL; 45 (LO RT), Sam Spicer/SS; 46 (CTR LE), BGSmith/SS; 46 (CTR RT), Ralph A. Clevenger/CO; 46 (LO LE), John Eastcott And Yva Momatiuk/NGC; 46 (LO RT), Johner Images/AL; 46 (UP), Patricio Robles Gil/NGC; 47 (UP RT), Ingo Arndt/MP/CO; 47 (UP RT), Alex Snyder; 47 (CTR LE), robert harding/AL; 47 (CTR RT), Paradise Picture/SS; 47 (LO LE), NG Maps; 47 (LO RT), Mark Raycroft/MP/NGC; Vocabulary box art (throughout), Baranovska Oksana/SS; Top border (throughout), Wiktoria Pawlak/SS

**National Geographic supports K–12 educators with ELA Common Core Resources.
Visit natgeoed.org/commoncore for more information.**

Table of Contents

Meet the Bears

Do you think you know all about bears? You might have a teddy bear or two. You might see bears on TV, in movies, or at a zoo.

But there are some things about bears that might surprise you.

Q Why do bears have fur coats?

A Because they would look silly in jackets!

brown bear in Glacier Bay National Park, Alaska, U.S.A.

Eight species of bear roam the world today. They are found on four continents. But each species looks and acts a little different from the others.

Let's meet the bears!

Den Notes

SPECIES: A group of closely related plants, animals, or other living things

5

What kind of bear do you picture when you think about bears? Maybe you think about polar bears. These snowy white bears live in the freezing Arctic. They are the biggest bears in the world.

polar bear in Svalbard, Norway

You might think of giant pandas, the black-and-white bears that live in China. They munch on bamboo all day.

giant panda

Maybe you think about black bears or brown bears. These two species are common in many places in North America. Some people can look out their window and see a black bear in their yard! Brown bears can be found in the forests of Asia, Europe, and North America. They're the most wide-ranging bears in the world.

weird but true!

Bears are faster than they look. A black bear can sprint 35 miles an hour for short distances.

You might not be as familiar with other kinds of bears.

Asiatic (ay-zhee-AT-ik) black bears are also called moon bears. They have a marking on their chest that looks like a crescent (KRES-unt) moon.

Asiatic black bear

sloth bear

Sloth bears have shaggy black hair. They look like they just rolled out of bed! They mainly live in India.

Sun bears are the smallest bears. They grow no heavier than a Great Dane dog. These bears are found in the tropical forests of Southeast Asia.

sun bear

Andean bears have only 13 pairs of ribs— one pair less than other bears.

Andean (AN-dee-uhn) bears have rings of white or golden fur around their eyes. That's why they're sometimes called spectacled bears. ("Spectacles" is another word for glasses.) They're the only bears native to South America.

Andean bear

Bears of the World

The world's eight bear species live in certain places around the globe. Check out the ranges of the world's bears.

Den Notes

 RANGE: The region (REE-juhn) where the animals of a particular species live

NORTH AMERICA

EUROPE

A S I A

ATLANTIC OCEAN

AFRICA

PACIFIC OCEAN

EQUATOR

PACIFIC OCEAN

SOUTH AMERICA

INDIAN OCEAN

AUSTRALIA

Bear Ranges

- American black bear
- Asiatic black bear
- Brown bear
- Giant panda
- Polar bear
- Sloth bear
- Andean bear
- Sun bear

ANTARCTICA

a black bear cub in a tree

a sun bear's claws

A bear's claws can grow as long as a white-board eraser.

Big Appetites

These grizzly bears in Alaska are catching fish.

Have you ever heard someone say "I'm as hungry as a bear"? That person must have been pretty hungry, because bears can eat a lot. Many types of bears eat anything they can find. Brown bears, black bears, and moon bears are omnivores. They eat grass, insects, fish, berries, garbage—you name it.

Polar bears live in an icy environment where few plants grow. So they mainly eat meat, such as seals and walruses. But like brown and black bears, a hungry polar bear will eat anything it can find.

Den Notes

OMNIVORE: An animal that eats both plants and animals

A polar bear drags a seal onto the ice.

Some bears are pickier eaters. Sloth bears and sun bears eat mostly insects, especially termites and ants.

All bears are considered carnivores. But pandas and Andean bears prefer to eat mostly plants! Pandas dine on just one type of plant—bamboo. Andean bears chow down on fruits and palms, and will even munch on corn in a farmer's field.

An Andean bear in Ecuador eats a grassy plant.

How Big Are Bears?

Bears need a lot of food to fuel their big bodies. Some are much heavier than humans. Polar bears weigh up to 1,800 pounds! Sun bears are tiny in comparison. They weigh up to 150 pounds. The sizes of all other bears fall in between. Let's see how bears compare.

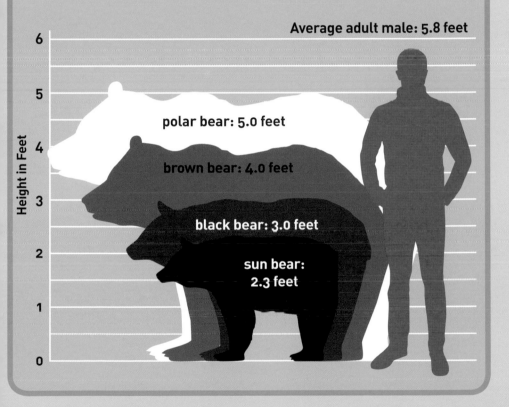

Average adult male: 5.8 feet

Height in Feet

polar bear: 5.0 feet

brown bear: 4.0 feet

black bear: 3.0 feet

sun bear:
2.3 feet

Den Notes

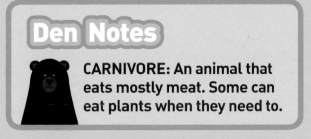

CARNIVORE: An animal that eats mostly meat. Some can eat plants when they need to.

Baby Bears

A giant panda holds her two-week-old cub.

Newborn panda cubs are the same size and weight as a stick of butter!

When bear cubs are born, mother bears have a big job. Newborn bears are helpless and tiny. They are blind and have almost no hair. Mother bears give the cubs everything they need. They keep the cubs warm and make sure they're safe and well fed.

Bears are mammals. So cubs drink milk from their mothers. The cubs grow and put on weight fast.

Den Notes

MAMMAL: An animal that produces milk to feed its young. Mammals usually have hair or fur covering their skin.

a polar bear mother and her three cubs

This is the first time out of the den for these polar bear cubs.

Weird but true!
A scientist once described polar bear milk as tasting like chalky, fishy cream. Yuck!

In colder areas, mothers give birth to cubs in a den. Cubs are often born in January or February. The cubs leave the den in March or April when they are big enough to travel. Cubs can't wait to get outside!

Den Notes

DEN: A shelter for a wild animal. Bear dens can be a hole in a hillside, a cave, or a burrow in a snowpack.

All bear cubs love
to goof around.
They tumble, chew,
and even swat at a
brother or sister. This helps
them practice skills they'll need to survive.

brown bear cubs playing

Bear cubs stay with their mother for one to
three years. She teaches them everything she
knows about how to live in the wild. Then
the cubs are ready to live on their own.

a grizzly bear
mother with
her cubs

6 COOL FACTS About Bears

A polar bear's hair isn't really white. It just appears that way because each hair is clear and hollow.

1

The biggest bear to ever live was the giant short-faced bear. Almost as tall as an elephant, this prehistoric bear died out between 500,000 and 2 million years ago.

2

Sloth bears have no front teeth. They use their mouth like a vacuum to suck up insects.

3

4

White spirit bears look like polar bears, but they're actually a rare kind of black bear.

5

A bear's sense of smell is seven times more powerful than a bloodhound's.

6

Many bear species often give birth to twins.

Super Sleepers

grizzly bear

When winter is coming, the temperature drops and food gets harder to find. What's a bear to do? Settle down for a long winter's nap, of course! Black bears and brown bears find a den and go into a sleeplike state for the winter. This is called hibernating.

Den Notes

HIBERNATE: To spend winter in a sleeplike state. This saves energy while there is little food available.

Not all bears hibernate. Bears that hibernate do it because there isn't enough food to survive the winter. For up to seven months, they don't eat, drink, or even take a bathroom break!

To prepare for their long sleep, bears eat as much as they can in the fall. The extra fat gives their bodies energy to survive until spring.

A Bear's Body

Bears have body parts with special abilities that allow them to stay healthy while they hibernate. Here are some cool features of a bear's body.

HEART: During hibernation, a bear's heart rate slows down. It goes from 60 beats per minute to 6 beats per minute. This saves energy. In the spring, the heart rate returns to normal.

black bear

BONES: If a person were to lie still for months, his or her bones would break down. But this doesn't happen to bears. When bears hibernate, a chemical in their bodies prevents bone breakdown. When bears wake up, their skeletons are still strong.

MUSCLES: A hibernating bear doesn't move much for months. In people, this would lead to muscle loss and severe weakness. But a bear's muscles stay strong.

There's much we don't understand about hibernating bears. How do their muscles stay strong after not moving for months? How do bears stay healthy after gaining so much weight and then nearly starving? Scientists are studying bears to try to answer these questions. Their findings might also be useful in treating human diseases.

A black bear mother and her cub hibernate in a den.

Weird but true!

To fatten up before hibernating, bears may eat 20,000 calories—or more—a day. That's like eating more than 65 cheeseburgers!

Q What's black and white, black and white, and black and white?

A panda rolling down a hill! **A**

Scientist Spotlight

Dave Garshelis (gar-SHELL-iss) risks life and limb by doing something many people consider crazy: entering a sleeping bear's den. Normally no one should ever disturb bears and their cubs. But Garshelis knows how to study them safely. He has special training and years of experience. He gives the mother bear a drug to make her sleep soundly. Then he and his team weigh the bears and take blood samples. The information helps the scientists learn more about bears and hibernation.

Garshelis (right) and his team run tests on a bear they drugged while it was hibernating. The bear lived longer than any known wild bear.

Don't Be Fooled!

These animals might sometimes be called bears, but they're not bears at all.

WATER BEAR (TARDIGRADE): Unlike bears, these critters are so small you almost need a microscope to see them. Tardigrades (TAR-dee-grades) are tiny creatures that live in moss and other wet places.

KOALA: If you ever hear people refer to koalas as "koala bears," feel free to politely correct them. A koala is a marsupial (mar-SOO-pee-ul), a type of animal with a pouch. They live in Australia, where there are no native bears.

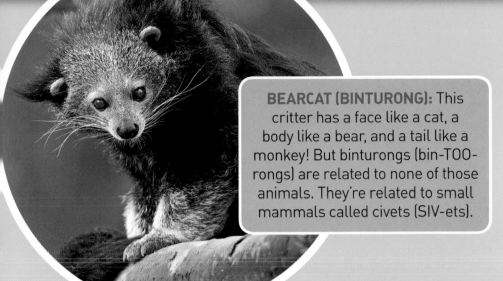

BEARCAT (BINTURONG): This critter has a face like a cat, a body like a bear, and a tail like a monkey! But binturongs (bin-TOO-rongs) are related to none of those animals. They're related to small mammals called civets (SIV-ets).

RED PANDA: Red pandas and giant pandas share similar names and live in the same region. But giant pandas are bears, while red pandas are not. The two species share a common relative that lived millions of years ago. But they're not very alike today.

Den Notes

MICROSCOPE: A tool for making very small objects and living things look bigger

Bears in Books

Bears have been popular characters in children's books for a long time. See how some beloved make-believe bears stack up against real-life bears.

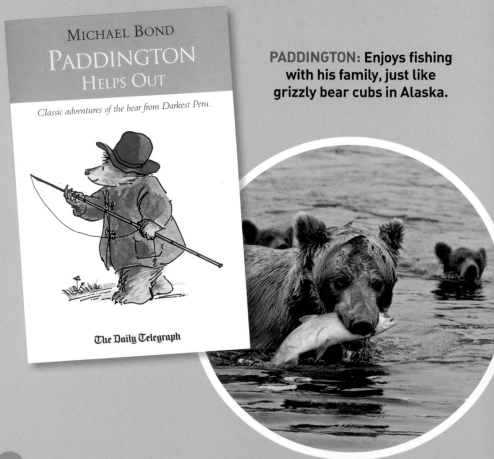

MICHAEL BOND

PADDINGTON
HELPS OUT

Classic adventures of the bear from Darkest Peru.

The Daily Telegraph

PADDINGTON: Enjoys fishing with his family, just like grizzly bear cubs in Alaska.

BALOO: Eats termites and ants, his favorite treats, just like a real sloth bear.

WINNIE THE POOH: Pooh Bear will do anything for honey, just like some real bears.

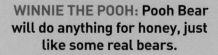

Bears and People

Prehistoric rock paintings from Chauvet Cave in France show bears and other animals.

People have had a special relationship with bears for thousands of years. Bears appear in famous cave paintings done by prehistoric people in France 30,000 years ago. Many other cultures also have lived alongside bears for a very long time.

A First Nations tribe in Canada has been teaming up with scientists to study bears. The tribe set up snares to snag bears' hair as they walked by. Scientists checked the DNA in the hair. They learned that a lot of bears go through the region to reach fish on the coast. Even the tribe didn't know so many bears traveled through the area.

A researcher collects bear fur.

It's easy to be in a place where bears live and have no idea that bears are there. That's because bears are good at avoiding people. With their powerful sense of smell, they know you're around long before you can see them.

Too Close for Comfort

If you're ever face-to-face with a bear, don't panic and don't try to run. Bears can run much faster than you. Instead, lower your eyes and back away in the direction you came from. A bear is likely to lose interest and walk away.

weird
but
true!

Bear attacks are extremely rare. A person would be more likely to get struck by lightning (and that's not very likely either!).

In Yosemite National Park in California, U.S.A., campers must put all food in special boxes.

Still, it's important to practice good bear manners when you're in bear country. The most important rule: Never leave food lying around. Hang food between trees at campsites. Use bear-proof garbage cans. If you spot a bear, keep your distance. Bears are aggressive only when they see you as a threat.

This old illustration shows a bear hunt in the Rocky Mountains.

Years ago, hunters often killed bears for their fur and meat. In some areas, bears were hunted until they nearly died out. Brown bears once lived all over western North America and into northern Mexico. But by the late 1880s, overhunting had wiped out most of them.

In Russia and parts of Asia, moon bear numbers may have dropped by half in the last 30 years. Overhunting is a major factor.

But there's hope for bears. In many parts of the world, laws protect endangered bears. Some places have rules that limit bear hunting. And experts have been working to protect bear habitats.

POLAR BEAR ALERT

STOP

DON'T WALK IN THIS AREA

Manitoba Conservation

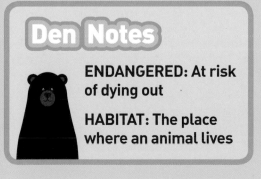

Den Notes

ENDANGERED: At risk of dying out

HABITAT: The place where an animal lives

POLAR BEAR ALERT

REPORT ALL BEARS TO 675-2327 (BEAR)

Manitoba Conservation

The Future for Bears

Like many animal species, bears face threats to their future. Some bears—such as sloth and sun bears—struggle from poaching and habitat loss. As people clear forests to get wood or to make farmland, bears have fewer places to live.

Den Notes

POACHING:
Illegal hunting

This forest in Canada is being cut down and cleared.

Melting sea ice means it's harder for polar bears to hunt.

Polar bears have a different problem. Because the climate is changing and the world is getting warmer, they have less sea ice to hunt on. Scientists agree that humans are playing a large role in the warming trend. Scientists are studying polar bears to see how they are handling their changing home.

A researcher dresses as a giant panda before he works with a cub.

For pandas, the problem is that only 1,600 remain in the wild. Pandas have the fewest numbers. At the Wolong Panda Reserve in China, a keeper slips into a panda suit. He disguises his scent. He's making sure the young panda cubs don't get used to humans as he teaches them how to survive in the wild.

This keeper and others want to boost panda numbers. But they are not the only ones working to help bears.

Panda Triplets

In 2014, the world celebrated a very special birth. Panda triplets were born at a safari park in China. It's rare for a panda to have triplets. Even more special—all three survived.

It's a Chinese tradition to name babies when they are 100 days old. So when the cubs turned 100 days old, they were given names in a special ceremony. Meet MengMeng (cute), KuKu (cool), and ShuaiShuai (handsome).

In Churchill, Canada, bears sometimes wander too close to town. In the past, such bears would have been killed. But now, workers return these bears to safety in the wild.

A polar bear looks into a research vehicle in Churchill, Canada.

Planting trees can help fight climate change.

It's up to us to make the world a place where bears and people can live together. There's so much you can do to help bears around the world. Here are a few ideas.

Learn all you can about bears. Books, magazines, and films are great sources. Visit your local library to find out more.

Go green! Fighting climate change helps all bears. Save energy by turning off electronics when you don't need them. Walk or ride your bike. Plant a tree.

Tell the bears' story. Create bear-related art or stage a play. You can sell tickets to your show. Later, donate the money to animal-welfare groups that work to protect bears.

Biking saves energy—and is a healthy way to travel!

QUIZ WHIZ

How much do you know about bears? After reading this book, probably a lot! Take this quiz and find out.

Answers are at the bottom of page 45.

Which of these continents does not have native bears?

A. Australia
B. North America
C. Asia
D. South America

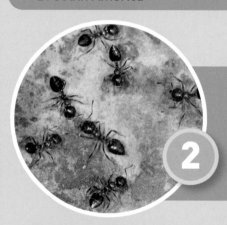

Which kind of bear loves to eat ants?

A. a sloth bear
B. a panda bear
C. a polar bear
D. an Andean bear

What does an omnivore eat?

A. only plants
B. only animals
C. both plants and animals
D. mostly plants with a few animals

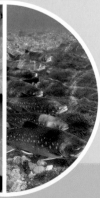

How do bears get ready to hibernate?

A. They get a lot of exercise.
B. They go on a diet.
C. They hide their food.
D. They eat a lot of food.

Which of these animals is really a bear?

A. a koala
B. a spirit bear
C. a water bear
D. a red panda

Where would you likely find a newborn bear cub in the winter?

A. in a den
B. in a tree
C. in a nursery
D. in its mother's pouch

Which species of bear has the fewest numbers in the wild?

A. sun bears
B. panda bears
C. brown bears
D. polar bears

Answers: 1. A; 2. A; 3. C; 4. D; 5. B; 6. A; 7. B

Glossary

CARNIVORE: An animal that eats mostly meat. Some can eat plants when they need to.

HABITAT: The place where an animal lives

HIBERNATE: To spend winter in a sleeplike state. This saves energy while there is little food available.

OMNIVORE: An animal that eats both plants and animals

POACHING: Illegal hunting

DEN: A shelter for a wild animal. Bear dens can be a hole in a hillside, a cave, or a burrow in a snowpack.

ENDANGERED: At risk of dying out

MAMMAL: An animal that produces milk to feed its young. Mammals usually have hair or fur covering their skin.

MICROSCOPE: A tool for making very small objects and living things look bigger

Bear Ranges
- American black bear
- Asiatic black bear
- Brown bear
- Giant panda
- Polar bear
- Sloth bear
- Andean bear
- Sun bear

RANGE: The region where the animals of a particular species live

SPECIES: A group of closely related plants, animals, or other living things

Index

Boldface indicates illustrations.